WIDE TO HIS WEATHER

WIDE TO HIS WEATHER

New Poems

by

Sister M. Paulinus Sullivan I.H.M.

and

Sister M. Davida Sullivan I.H.M.

THE GOLDEN QUILL PRESS
Publishers
Francestown   New Hampshire

International Standard Book Number 8233-0195-8

Library of Congress Catalog Card Number 73-86532

Printed in the United States of America

Nihil Obstat:
MONSIGNOR JAMES T. CLARKE
Censor Librorum
February 22, 1973

Imprimatur:
✠ J. CARROLL McCORMICK
Bishop of Scranton
February 22, 1973

Dedication

For the Immaculate Heart of Mary,
Perennially Open to His Weather.

Acknowledgment

Some of these poems have already appeared in the following periodicals: *America, Commonweal, Lyric, Spirit, The Catholic World and the Sign.* We thank the editors for permission to reprint.

Contents

I

Out of my peace
I will sing You
A song of green growth
Holding golden fulfillment.

"A CERTAIN SLANT OF LIGHT"

Spare daylight mantles trees
And life. All, all is sorrowful November.
Dreams shiver in thin tweeds of umber,
Tan and taupe and leaden grey. Memories

Come dun-clad in the failing fall:
The self-same memories that in the spring
Raced swift forsythia in games of mingling
Gold and young chartreuse today assume all

Autumn's ochre. But see! A certain slant of light
Slides sudden through the Munsell indigos,
Slants uncertain — certain — lustres rows
Of oak, leaf-littered lawn, and swallow flight.
My heart, remember these brown velvet glows
Of late November, this blue-fire flight of crows.

Sister M. Davida

HUSBANDRY

Not a finger have I laid on grain
Or gourd or pumpkin,
Yet I am busy enough with autumn,
Garnering, gathering in.

Against the day of dearth, the hoar
And frugal hour,
Not body alone, but heart and mind as well
Have need of store.

And so I am cellaring, memory-deep,
For the mind and the heart to keep,
Color and tang, each texture and shape, call
Of this bird and that, all, all
That I may of Beauty's yield
On the witching weald
Of sumptuous fall.

Sister M. Paulinus

THE ROCOCO POCONOS

Each Pocono
flaunts rococo
the Indians
treasured long ago.

The Poconos
are full of does
and setting suns
of gold and mauves.

Locofoco Poconos
rim round plateaus
with fiery trees
of flame and rose.

And in the snows
still Poconos
look down through stars
on glass plateaus.

Where go the mighty Poconos
when mist up from the valley flows
at times? It seems
that no one knows.

Sister M. Davida

AND WINDS SNOW–WEIGHTED RIDE

Prayer, I have imaged so:
Glistening and white and deep
And drifting still
Through waking hours and sleep.
How long,
O Lord of the Drift,
How long shall prayer
But barely sift
Here where the heart is wide
To Your weather
And winds, snow-weighted ride?

Sister M. Paulinus

LAUDATE IN LINDISFARNE

Standing in the rime-wave up to his breast
Cuthbert of Melrose calls on the rest
Of God's creatures there in the night
To praise Him with forthright
Billows of song.

Better than ever David might,
This English monk,
Brother to wind and frost and night,
To ice and snow, as Francis to the sun,
Spearheads the run of antiphon.

Hail and hoarfrost praising the Lord,
Cold an undiminishing chord,
Chant of the wind, crag in its mouth,
And the voice of the sea, wave against rock,
Crashing response. Then cock-

Crow — and Cuthbert walking the sand
With two small seals snug at his feet,
For the God of the psalms is a kingly king,
And quick in kindness to those who sing
His praise athwart the windy dark
Of Northumbrian night and the stark
Rime-cold of the sea.

Sister M. Paulinus

COSMIC CHRISTMAS

Let us not be afraid in all this drift
Of stars. Let us not bog in dunes of thought.
Though modern man, now come of age and taught
Responsibility, has passed the space-craft

Driver's test, let us not faint in awe
Of this near rush of stars and giddy self-
Possession. We rocket from this conscious shelf
Not wholly on our own, but radar led through law

And love, to keep our rendezvous with evolution.
Snow and stars now drift toward the divine,
And, autonomous as seems our flight, the flow of time
Is tide that draws us in a Taoist tangent to our
          revolution.

Through this white cosmic night go gay and brave
As other wise men lead us to the lighted cave.

Sister M. Davida

THE GOOD NEWS REBORN
(To Man, the "Soaring Arrow
of the Great Biological Synthesis")

Announce to Mao, to Brezhnev, Sartre, and Cæsar
A way out of the Cosmic cold. The news that's missed
By many cubs and many commentators is just this:
The Gospel story is still relevant. We freeze — or

Warm our hearts with this: True frames
Of reference, axes, differing dimensions,
Alien horizontals, harmonies, and tensions
Hold a radiance that touches Personality, that flames

From hearths not solely solar kindled, but lit by Hands
That clasp our human ones in strengths and sympathies
The heart and mind of mankind since his infancy
Has thrilled to. Not understanding, we seek to
      understand:

Once more find man the focal point of Godly aim,
Creation point, the Incarnation point, to whom He
      came.

Sister M. Davida

RESPONSE

"Sing me a song," you said,
"To lift my heart."
And so my fragile art
Dares reach to where
Our Lady lifts a Child
Who lifts the world.
She is the muted exquisite music,
He the limitless Word
Of Joy.
And you — oh fortunate you,
Exult, exult,
For you have heard.

Sister M. Paulinus

GIFTS
(A Nun Makes Final Vows)

It took three Orient kings to bring to Him
What you bring unobtrusively today:
Gold, frankincense, and myrrh.
(And symbol is less than what it signifies.)

Wisdom and wealth together planned
This truly worshipful outlay of kings
Who nevertheless came home to stores
Lessened but little by their regal gifts.
But you who purpose no return withhold
No jot of myrrh, of frankincense, of gold.

Sister M. Paulinus

CYBERNATION

What calculus
of wind and cold
and light and timing
and terrain, to bend this violet
curve of snow, while all the olive afternoon
the college IBM's click merely miles of student grades!

Sister M. Davida

BEFORE EXUBERANCE OF BIRDS

They will come again, this spring,
(Please God!) as they always do:
Robin and blue-bird, song-sparrow,
Thrush and warbler and vireo:
Soloist and choristers will know
How to fling and float and whirl and swirl
Music as daring and as shy as April light.

But here and now (with no disparaging
Of birds in windfall) I praise in common justice,
Before exuberance of birds shall come our way,
The brave lone bird —
Woodpecker, perhaps, or cardinal or nuthatch —
Who lifts our winter-weary hearts at intervals
With spring, the length of a note —
Or a streak of notes,
Snow still on the mountains, and dearth
Everywhere on the Lentscaped earth.

Sister M. Paulinus

QUERY

From freshman through senior college classes,
I taught this ordinary girl.
Or was she so?
She showed me her engagement ring last evening.
Light, brighter than her diamond, tapered to
      her finger tips.
All radiance, all holiness,
This — oh, this most extraordinary girl
Stood strangely against familiar desks,
      blackboards and maps.
How had I erred so widely in estimating her?
Or had I?
Love, I have long known, works miracles.

Sister M. Paulinus

ANNUNCIATION

Angels are metaphors,
The scripture scholars say.
I like it either way.
If man can think an angel — even seraphim —
Well, good for man, oh very good for him!

        *   *   *

Ablaze with angelhood
Great Gabriel stood
Before the girl
(His overshadowing wings
Like to great golden harps)
And he announced to her
That God's high wish
To make her mother of His Son
Awaited her consent.

And the girl's answer, awed and low,
Shimmered into his wings:
"Be it done unto me according to thy word."
And her whisper sounded in heaven,
Throughout all heaven,
Like to a smiting of strings
Such as no harp had ever borne
Or ever would or could.

Sister M. Paulinus

CANTICLE IN AN ORANGE GROVE

Be as a row of Eucalyptus,
God,
Before my threatened blossoming;
Rebuff whatever blasts
Prepare to ride
All blissful blooming down.

Be windbreak, God,
And I will praise You
With golden fruits.
Out of my peace,
I will sing You
A song of green growth
Holding golden fulfillment.

Sister M. Paulinus

OF MOUNTAIN LAUREL

Mountain laurel is delightfully indigenous.
(Hail to the Pennsylvania law
That keeps it in the mountains!)
There are shrubs in plenty elsewhere
Calling out to be potted for sick rooms,
For transplanting in back and front yards,
And for Memorial Day tributes.

The traveler through the Endless Mountains,
(And what mountains are not endless?)
Under the sky that is always there,
Through gregarious green,
Welcomes the suave yet simple relief
Of this sprint of pinkness,
Always a glad surprise,
Yet not entirely unexpected,
As a buck or a doe along the self-same route
Is both somewhat expected and a surprise.

And mountain laurel suggests that God has enjoyed
Dashing some charm into His making
Even where He has hurled the mountains into place
And taken responsibility for the forest.

Sister M. Paulinus

NOR IN THE EYE OF THE BEHOLDER

I did not create the red-wing blackbird.
Imagination could not feign that flash
    beneath the wing.
Another Artist must have struck that flame
    from tree to crust.
An Artist who designed a Sabbath for His leisure
    to observe such hidden things
Must have concealed that red beneath the
    blackbird's wings for His own pleasure.

Sister M. Davida

AS ANY LOVER MIGHT

You are constrained, being in love with God,
To revel in His workmanship,
As any lover might, confessing the beloved.
You note with praise the nuanced interplay
Of light with shade, the way a river curves;
Sighting a swan handsome in black
With beak of regal scarlet
Moving with beauties that wear accustomed white
And beaks of usual gold,
You catch your breath at God's command of drama.
Delighting in His versatility, you drink His varied air,
Elate with mint or kind with thyme or clover.

You rest adoringly
In stillness standing against the stars.

* * *

Being in love, you think in terms of love.

Sister M. Paulinus

SONG OF SURPRISE

"The hollyhocks look so surprised," you said to me,
Brightening your garden further with your glance.
You were not conscious that your speech was poetry,
Nor were you in the least aware

That you yourself might be a cause of fair
Surprise. But oh, your children, we
Your children knew. Ever your selflessness freshly
Revealed itself before our wondering eyes.

Ever we were discovering anew
That all the eminently wise
And so important things we learned abroad
We somehow knew before in knowing you.

Heaven-deep in white surprise now may you be,
Who while you lived evoked it winsomely.

Sister M. Paulinus

SPACE AGE SONNET TO THE MOON

Sophisticated poets sing of atom dust
And Freud and stuffed refrigerators. How dare
I in this Great Society salute the fair
And gabble of the moon? But must is must.

Will Shakespeare marked "How sweet the moonlight
     sleeps
Upon this bank!" and Sidney "even of fellow-
Ship" could write. "In silver shoon" did de la
Mare once follow her. While Keats in "gules" steeped

All the Isle of Wight. Archibald MacLeish claims
Poetry "is motionless in time
(Twice, "motionless in time") as the moon climbs."
And Frost spread out a homely apron to the same.

Cool Cynthia, saluted by the poets' song
Through silvered centuries, timidly we join the throng.

Sister M. Davida

SAPPHO SO EMPLOYED

Hanging fresh linen on a line
In buoyant weather — or benign —
Is lyricism unalloyed.
Sappho so employed,
Bending low and reaching high
Against a Grecian sky,
(Clear in the Grecian way
And bluer far than ours, they say)
Sappho, reaching arms and face
Towards the sun's embrace,
Sunlight lilting through her hair,
Linen lilting in the air,
And her fingers and her form
Lightly busy with a norm
Of movement, patterned, yet shot-through
With spontaneity —
Bird-song all about —
Sappho so, there is no doubt,
Had outrivaled, myriad lines of linen ago
The lyric Sappho that we know.

Sister M. Paulinus

WAKING

I

Thunder in the treetops —
and bells there too.
A lifting of branches and hearts —
the pneuma arrives.

II

Memories of attic rooms—huge, empty, endless—
　　　　and curtains flaring in the wind.
An echo in the wall of the subconscious!
Ariadne! Ariadne!

III

A fear has happened, will happen,
is lurking in the shadow caves of psyche.
What awful thing has happened,
will hap, perhaps, today?
Tread not my labyrinths to sleuth
the shriek that wakened thunder in the treetops.

IV

Breathe soft. Chime sky and bells.
For it is over. Or is it over?
Over, yes. But never real.
O never real calamity, how blissful that you
　　　　never happened!
Benovolent the bells within the treetops.
We lift our hearts with lifting of the branches.

Sister M. Davida

TRIPLE "THANK YOU"

Watching in mind, with reverent awe,
(As who did not?)
Our astronaut, settling his camera
Solidly in air —
And leaving it there,
There came also into my view
Brigid, Abbess of Kildare,
A.D. four hundred fifty-two.
There she was, hanging up her cloak,
With decorum and gayety,
Not on a peg, not on an oak,
But (however outer-spacey it may seem)
On a sunbeam.

I thank the legend-maker for this fancy;
John Glenn, for the sheer event;
And for relishing of both,
God, Whose giving is never spent.

Sister M. Paulinus

THE FURTHEST STAR

"I'm not shying any more,
Not any more. I'm talking,"
The three-year-old confided.
Bravo, dear child, bravo!
Yet do not let all shyness go.

(O speech sweeter than song
Of hummingbird or robin!
O withdrawnness wooing me
Endearingly!)

Speak freely, child, and happily;
Yet be a little shy.
As you grow older you will know
That shyness is lily of the valley,

Mignonette, forget-me-not,
A deft, unworldly doe
A name for winsomeness,
The furthest star.

Sister M. Paulinus

II

A backdrop fit for sorrow, this pearl morning

FOR DIANE —
A TEN YEAR OLD SPINAL BIFIDA

Stone-stubbed, the Gentile and the Jew —
face downward fallen on a rock.
Diana, lovely stone of stumbling —
lucid-eyed, slender-faced, suffering Diane —
Platonic sage, assembling life through television
        shadows —
pale, water-lily of a child adrift
upon a trundle bed—white flame-flower on a lily pad—
all disembodied, all literally disembodied,
almost all literally — face and shoulders,
arms and twining hands these ten years tied
in pain to roots too shrunken to be called a body . . .

Stone-stubbed are Greek and Jew —
face downward fallen on a rock.
Diana at our crossroads, where wistful portholes
open out of pain, and television windows flash
a twisted picture of the world! ("It's not
the focusing," explains Diane. "It's just this channel.")
Pallid goddess, coursing stags of pain, to Jews
frustration and to Gentiles foolishness —
Diane at our crossroads, where beauty and the whirling
        world
meet faith and pain — Diana, darling . . .

Diane is dead.
The pined years die away
like ripples where a stone has fallen in still water —
or like a water lily folded in the night.

Sister M. Davida

MISSING IN ACTION

*(For Captain John B. Sullivan, III, U.S.A.F., Missing
in Action over North Vietnam, June 21, 1966. Also
for His Parents.)*

With exquisite sensitivity and fondness
He played the scores of Chopin, Beethoven, Bach,
  Mozart;
Then fashioned scores himself with strong and subtle
  art.

And with equal fondness and sensitivity
He studied planes, climbed skies as he climbed scales.
"He takes our ships faster and farther up
Than veterans do," Air Force personnel reported,
Stopping a casual moment at his university.

His father and his mother brave it out,
Hoping, still hoping, he is alive and coming home,
Yet fearing for him many an hour and day;
And sometimes, they surmise,
That from the freedom of the skies
Into the sheer and shining freedom of God's arms,
He plummeted.

Sister M. Paulinus

MEKONG MOON
(Post-War Lullaby)

Mekong Moon, walking through the rice fields,
Bear gently the heroic dead upon their shields
      to Avalon.

Mekong Moon, melting bombed out towns to a
      macabre loveliness,
Melt bayonet and tank and barbed wire ugliness.

Tangle moonbeams in the fingers of our little ones;
Light lives and dreams of these unwanted sons
      of Mars and Helen.

Mekong Moon, untangle hatred, intrigue, lies;
Mold planes and bombs to stillness; hush skies to
      lullabies.

Heartsick and wounded ones, sooth with your
      silver salves.
For lost and imprisoned sons gild homeward paths
      from Babylon.

Mekong Moon, silvering enamels of your dark
      cloisonné,
Join maps and mythologies in exquisite play.

Sister M. Davida

RAIN

A backdrop fit for sorrow, this pearl morning!
How nobly patient seem these ancient trees
That wear the mist like ragged sleeves
And bow to last night's storm.

A fitting trope for sorrow, this pale music!
In the almost silence of the dripping rain
There throbs the universal pulse of pain
From Eve's revolt till now.

Yielding to this measure,
We synchronize our ache
With this great universal ache,
Wrench pliable the rod

That rises so unyielding
In the midst of us, and crush
It in the beauty of this dove-lustrous
Dawn.

Sister M. Davida

EULOGY FOR PLAINSONG

The melody flows on; let it erode.
Through granite, salt, whatever else
Man's heart becomes at death's fixed stare,
This stream of chant wears paths to solace.
This music of the clear, continuous stream
Carves valleys, furrows farms of fairness
In the rock of sorrow. Let melody erode.

Sister M. Davida

OF A MAY EVENING

Lilacs and lilac shades and greens of gloom,
Rain-washed sun on far, grey, eastern buildings —
Why should not a maiden lady, age seven
      o'clock, of a May evening
Borrow a lilac teacup of deep green loneliness
This hour when May devotions suddenly are
      abolished?

Sister M. Davida

SEPARATION

Close-knit by blood, they chat across a tiny room,
The while whole continents of mind and heart loom
Dark between; their casual numerous words
Tangle to jungles breeding ominous birds,
The while the canary sings,
And the afternoon sun flings
Blood-warming gold
Across the intimate threshold.

And I am glad that only the sea
Stretches between my kin and me.

Sister M. Paulinus

O FIRST AMONG YOUNG HEROES, CHRIST
(For John Fitzgerald Kennedy)

The ancient English had a name
For You, O Christ, bright as their curls
Of gold, their cups, their rings, a name that hurls
Itself upon our hearts with instant and incisive claim
This dirge-filled distant day.

Honoring this suitability, precise and fair
And strong, we cry You now —
And vigorously — by this, Your name of earliest
     English fame:
(Let it echo through our air, echo, echo brightly there)
"Young Hero, Hero, O."

Between the Humber and the Thames, above, below,
They hailed You so,
Forthrightly hastening to confess
You met their tests of leadership:
Bravery and comeliness and bright and bold largesse.

Humbly, this latter day, we make our plea:
One who has likewise trysted with these three —
Largesse and comelinss and bravery —
And unto death — even as You,
Comes to Your heavenly company.

O First among Young Heroes, Christ,
Receive him well,

Who was "Your man," indeed,
Bone of the bone, core of the core of the hero-breed.
"Your man," who swore You fealty "one shining
        hour,"
And shiningly forebore
(Come ambushed hate, come malice, come the absurd)
To break his noble word.

Sister M. Paulinus

IN MEMORIAM
(USA, November, 1963)

Six grey, apocalyptic horses draw the caisson
with the flag-draped coffin of an antic death
along a swath of sunlight and then along a swath
of shade. So motionless its motion, it is as though
eternity rolls there along an endless avenue;
and mostly left and left and left of feet
and white-gloved hands that move like synchronized,
white pendulums are all that yet remain of time,
together with the thrum of muffled, rolling drums.

Tragedy complete in its catharsis has grouped
the chastened crowd in blocks and circles, triangles
and rectangles — whatever way space bends.
A nation droops in silence as the body of its leader
passes by. Not a muscle of a soldier's face relaxes;
not an eyelid winks; no grey November twig
rubs on another twig. Restive alone, the horse
all riderless. Empty and inverted stirrups
flap undisciplined against his sides. Restive
the horse, all riderless.

Sister M. Davida

DOUBLE–PARKED

In the cold daylight of fifty-five
You see it there when the traffic halts.
It is not what you thought it was in the rush,
        not what you thought.
"Choose what you thought! Choose!"
Shouts the traffic cop, while drivers
Grind their brakes and screech foul lullabies.
"Choose to live with it or join the rush again!"

Sister M. Davida

REMEMBERED PRELUDE
(On Leaving Home to Become a Nun)

How I waited when a child
Eagerly, for the sound
Of his step
On the asphalt, on the stair;
And with what a bound
Of bliss, I found
His arms, claimed his kiss.

Later, there came an evening
When I waited with growing dread
For his step.
Briskly, as usual, it came along the walk,
And he stood there in the doorway,
Pleasant and lithe and princely,
And he said,
"So you're leaving us, my dear."

My father, O my father,
Why did you have to force
Such carefully casual cheer
Into your voice before it broke?

Sister M. Paulinus

O GENTLE RAIN, DOWN POUR

The hot stones in my river beds are dry.
Gnats cloud my sweetest fruit and snare
Each darling of a whispered wind.
Leaves waken in the belfries of the trees
And rain slides into August.

Sister M. Davida

III

Surf fingering the morning light with wonder

MOON TORSION

In years I have not yielded so to moonlight.
See me, bent here, twisted like some wire
Baroque, and all from following the frost of fire
That plays from middle left to upper right

Of my pale window. Like threads of music, shreds
Moon-mesh the eaves, the firs, and trawl
My memory for nights I lay enthralled
In peonies and honeysuckle and hibiscus. Then heads

Of national commissions held no schemes to shove
Off for the moon, to rendezvous, to moor. The moon
Was not a place; it was for tides and lunar
Time and silvering the night to stillness and for love —
It was, as now, for casting all the world
To peaks of awe in silence numinous as thunder furled.

Sister M. Davida

THESE ARE YOUR YEARS
(A Nun Celebrates Her Silver Jubilee)

These are your years: lilt
Of light, lilt of waves,
Surf fingering the morning light
With wonder.
And then (tempo accelerando)
Upsurge against all dark,
Upsurge towards stars
That breast the æons
Or glow with new-breed quest,
Silver that answers silver
With high-surf hardihood,
Silver aglimmer with God.

Sister M. Paulinus

THE PRISTINE POISE

The blueness, when God poised the fountains,
First glistened with your gracious words:
        Joy poured abroad —
            Balanced blue waters
        At play before God.

In the roseness as God launched His first gliding gulls,
The waves rested, dreaming of your gentle hands:
        Still gulls in motion —
            Frail equilibrium
        Smoothing the ocean.

Oh, the world in its fullness of beauty
Carolled songs of your pristine grace, sang:
        "Honey Steeped Noonlight,
            Mater Amabilis,
        Valley All Moonbright."

Then the new Sabbath steadied to silence
As God loved an all-loving world,
And in blueness love poised as in Mary:
        Silk doves in their nest —
            Love of God and God's love
        In serene silken rest.

Sister M. Davida

FOR THE DEDICATION OF A CHAPEL

Girders can sing:
O strong, strong
Their lifted song;
Wood, be it understood,
Was once a tree
And remembers lyrically.
Radiant
The choral phrase
Light and glass together raise.

O glow, glow
Voice of the wood, voice of the steel,
Voice of the many-colored glass, glow
And grow to brilliant crescendo.
Praise Him, O nuanced notes,
O structured song, praise
Him
To Whom the choirs
Of Heaven rear,
In tier on singing tier,
Their glorious trisagion.

Sister M. Paulinus

APPLAUSE IN THE AULA

Weary from travel, dusty from the road,
Breathing heavily in heat-hung hall,
Apostles on the Eve of Pentecost — so
Met Vatican II. Pope John knelt,
Weighted down with eighty years of care
And nineteen hundred years of regimentals.
Then slowly, solemnly, he rose, and the barriers
Went down before his smile. Babel's Tower
Toppled with his handshake. He thrust
Aside the trappings of his office, and, striding
Through the hearts he'd flung so wide,
Walked (not was carried)
Across the council chamber of the Trinity;
And the aula of the heavens roared applause.

John XXIII leaned
Out from heaven as formerly he'd leaned
To greet his relatives on coronation day.
Down an avenue of years he pointed to the Church
In all her glory: Dun tarnish
And the dust of travel through dim centuries,
Byzantine pomp, baroque embarrassment
Were doffed with all the ease with which
he'd doffed his cope.
And Christ stood in a boat with Peter:
Muscles gleamed in Galilean sun,
And Galilean water splashed the farthest

Corners of the world as bronzed, young
Fishermen drew in their nets —
New, strong, shining nets,
That broke not with the catch miraculous.

John pointed to the Church in all her glory:
Another vision of the New Jerusalem
Another John had dreamed about.
And all the aula thundered with applause!

Sister M. Davida

THE GREAT ADVENTURE

With siren flourish and with flashing lights
   the ambulance draws to a halt across the road.
The faithful cross themselves; the faithless manage
     studied nonchalance.
Oh to meet death as the great adventure!
Not to "rage against the night"
   nor go "as quarry slave scourged to his dungeon"
     nor yet to leave as one who "draws the drapery of
       his couch about him."
Not to go fearfully as toward a casqued knight on an
     armored steed,
  nor yet carelessly as on vacation,
    but with high hope mounting to sheer exaltation.

Sister M. Davida

PSALM OF PRAISE UPDATED

Praise the Lord,
You galaxies, a hundred billion shy
Before His Face, each, each with singing reach
Wrought of a hundred billion stars.
Crash, crash His Name abroad, thunder
On massive thunder.
Exult earth and firmament;
Trumpet His triumph,
Spheres and stratosphere,
All outer-space, extol Him.

Men of the new science,
Turning amazing keys in amazing doors,
Praise Him,
First Cause of all your sight and insight.
Voyagers to the moon,
Go out before Him, exploring the work of His Hands,
Widening our glimpse of His glory,
And, coming in, splash down
His inscrutable Name.

Sister M. Paulinus

THE KINGDOM OF HEAVEN
(*Choral Introductions for a Music Program*)

I

The Kingdom of Heaven
Is like a Christmas morning:
It sings like a carol within us.
It is the clear, high note of a bell,
Riding like a star
Before the blue ebb of night.
It is a near, bright star
Ringing like a silver bell
To greet the morning light.
Oh, heaven is joy
In the court of a Boy;
It is mirth
Brought to earth
By hope at Christ's birth.
It is goodwill like cascades of daylight within us.
It is chimes of God's will like bright bell notes within
      us.
It is silver bells in us, high, high within us.

II

The Kingdom of Heaven
Is like an August afternoon
Upon a wooded mountainside,
Where song like slender tendrils
Climbs the sunlight
Through the trees;
Where strong, green vines like trills
Of fragile bird-song
Swing upon the breeze.
Heaven is God in His Sacrament of Love
Binding hearts together
With tough tendrils grown above.
Oh heaven is love like summer afternoon within us;
It is God's love reaching out like green vines from
        within us.
It is flute trills within us, far, far within us.

III

And sometimes in the world
We find that heaven is like
The coming on of night within us:
A strong, green tide of twilight
Like a cello
In a symphony;
The cool, deep flowing of a cello
Like green twilight
From the eastern sea.
Heaven is at times a strain
Of music from taut strings of pain
Deep, deep within us.
It is the Comforter resolving pain to minor chords of
        harmony within us.

IV

And in the world to come
We'll find "eye has not seen
Nor ever ear has known,
Nor has it entered human hearts
What thing God has prepared
For those who love Him."

Sister M. Davida

IV

With vectors, points, parabolas
and astute gerrymandering on maps
the weatherman traced temperatures,
tornadoes, pressure highs and lows,
prevailing winds and tides.

DREAMS OF THE MOBILE ARTIST

I
STRUCTURE

Poor Fernando!
Long he labored
to create an art without an art —
to structure the unstructured.
Blue on white on green on purple oils he squandered.
"Surge, O Sea, in iridescent opal;
banish boundaries; eliminate all limitation."
But arching foot on crest succeeding perfect crest,
the moon maintained an ancient matriarchy.
Poor Fernando!
impoverished by canvas fit to rig a clipper,
soothed by moonlight,
fettered to a frame.

BALANCE

The swimming ballerinas,
gloved in black,
in faultless evening dress,
wove back and forth
through music and the wandering lights
completely free and fleeting.
What groomed divinity!
disdainful both of wooing vertical
and wavering horizontal,
but wedded to a discipline of breath
and thigh and finny feet!
"Oh balance of glissading ballerinas,
perfect mobile free of filament!'
exclaimed the artist,
and wound his arms about the goldfish bowl —
and waked.

III
Precision

"Sun sets today at 5:05;
tomorrow, 8:01 it rises."
With vertors, points, parabolas,
and astute gerrymandering on maps
the weatherman traced temperatures,
tornadoes, pressure highs and lows,
prevailing winds and tides.
Mat, the Mobile Artist, gaped at this precision;
but mankind, cloyed by marvels and martinis,
swayed TV rockers to and fro
and filled up this exciting TV "pause"
with talk, just talk, or turned it off
while Hurricane Alecto buzzed above antennas.

IV
DIS-STRUCTURE

Thrice forty years they swung there
     with a tick and a tock:
classrooms lined with row on row
      a-giggle or a-gape
       from nine to three o'clock;
block on block of offices, a-click
       with castanets of stenographic senoritas
       from nine to five o'clock;
brokers slung from ticker tape
       from ten to two
       with tick and tock.
Thrice forty years they floated there
adrift among the skyscrapers and steeples
adrift above the boulevards and clover leaves
and other whirling peoples
convinced of motion in æternam.
Snip, went Mat the Mobile Artist, tired of his design.
Boys and girls and stockbrokers are waiting in a line
       with senoritas.

Sister M. Davida

BEGGARY

No voice to raise in suppliancy,
No hands for beggary's outstretched palms,
Nor any knee for falling upon,
Had I on whom You showered alms.

Here was beggary bleak indeed:
Only a possible being I,
Until You stooped and mercifully decreed
Me life. Then let me look
Respectfully on every lesser lack
Of every kind,
And succor as I may the merely lame,
The merely deaf or blind.

Sister M. Paulinus

POINT FOR SCRIBE AND PHARISEE

Amazingly He smote; abrupt and hard His blow:
"It is not good to take the children's bread and throw
It to the dogs."

       Disarmingly sure
Her foil: "Yea, Lord, even the whelps have fare
Of crumbs let fall."

           "O practiced Scribe and Pharisee,
What think you of this Canaanite's command of
      repartee?
How often you have gnashed your teeth, seeing how
      dim
Your prowess shone against a glint of argument
Splintering about your heads! And this the consequent
Of dialectic steel dealt agilely by Him
Of Nazareth!"

       Fencers whose striving is futility,
Observe: His thrust is parried by humility

Sister M. Paulinus

SONNET TO LIFE
(On reading Teilhard de Chardin)

One should not have gone there. A bus that speaks
Five languages, a cab, a plane, the metro
Are locale for tourist babble. My friends I let go
With the guide and browsed into a bookstall. Drab
      deeps

Led down through labyrinthine thought, absurd
As twilit trenches feeling out their way! The dark
(My enemy! My friend!) hid horrors of a world of war
Cased there to carbonate — a skull, a bayonet, a word-

Crazed radio, debris of post-war dry disgust.
Of course I had my freedom. In that tunnel, I alone
Was master. I could lie still and moan
Or wriggle on revoltingly through mounds of dust.

A pick-point rent the roof and Teilhard,
White with wisdom, handed in the daystar.

Sister M. Davida

O SHADE OF MICHAEL'S SWORD ABROAD
(For Any Contemplative)
"Be still and see that I am God." — *Psalm XLV*

Demon of Duplicity, for once
His aim is single: to rout
All inner quiet (He can't afford to care
Just now what you may fret about).

He has a growing fear,
Observing you of late,
That what has happened before
May happen again — and here.

For all your ordinariness,
You call for topskill wariness —
He's seen your kind before:
The kind who could be really still,

And so could really see,
According to the promise,
(O shade of Michael's sword abroad!
O gross calamity!)

That God is really God.

Sister M. Paulinus

POTPOURRI

All this jangle, crash, and rumble
Of the world in pieces falling,
All this wild, chaotic jumble
Has our dendrites set on edge.

What a polyglot!
Books and books, a million
Or a trillion
Or a quinta-quadra-billion,
And all so ably written
As to turn your head around
And around
And round.

It's puzzling, it is; I mean it.
The world's too big for me
And too little for what's in it.

What a flock of treaty papers!
Not a flock,
But flocks
And flocks
Of flocks.

And the state of things!
Why a nation is a nation
And in six or seven hours

It's a cluttered railway station
For a lord that growls and lowers.

There's too much of many things.
And then the awful break-up:
States and thoughts
And even atoms
And the great white peace
For which we fought the wars
We hear breaking, breaking, breaking
Into bits
Into nothings
Into naughts.

And some of us will whirl with them,
And try to catch them all,
And be broken in the fall —
Go mad with dizziness and dancing
And the fear of breaking things.

And some will let them go,
Let them go;
Let the pieces mean no more
Than the tick
Of many clocks,
Than the click
Of ivory chessmen
And the variegated blocks
That children scatter;

Than the chink
Of ice in glasses
And the clink
Of foreign coins
And the patter, patter,
Patter of the rain.

And some will build with them
And make the most of them;
Fall deeper, deeper, deep
In the mightiness of God
The Master-builder,
Who gathers all the pieces
As they jangle, crash, and rumble,
As they tick and click
And chink and clink.
As they scatter —
Pitter, patter —
He who built the world from nothing
Builds the world again anew
Of bits of emerald
And vermilion
And gold
And blue
And — blue.

Sister M. Davida

MARGINALIUM

The allegorist who was Bede looked on
Approvingly as Bede, the chronicler,
Studded the page with sudden pearls. Such were
They found, the chronicler made note, upon
These coasts: crimson and white and others yet
Of purple, green or lustrous violet;
And here, I think, Bede, the historian, let fall his quill,
While Bede who loved an allegory smiled,
Urbanely pleased, as shining figures filed
Across his peace. "Gracious is God's high will,"
He mused. "These are the pearls of white in truth,
Monks of this house and holy Weremouth. Here
      Eosterwine
And Ceolfrid, here kings of ancient line
Flashed far the light of purple pearls. Red glow
In pearl the brave who letter manuscripts
Despite our numbing frost and snow.
Gracious is God. Praise to His name. Amen."
And Bede took up his chronicler's quill again.

Sister M. Paulinus

"A CLEAN WELL–LIGHTED PLACE"

Crow-caw and rust-red bird;
snake on the stone at the water's edge; a cry
in the August afternoon, a slowing car, strange
music and the eerie dance and incantation of unfamiliar
worship. A front page forest full
of violent and occult crimes that creep along
the edges of the century — and then this auburn sunset.
Gratefulness goes up like incense
from this clean, well-lighted place.

Dark — and a terrific pouring — Lake Erie
Merely Lake Erie and the wind and darkness!
What power in this pouring, in this gloom. And Lake
        Erie
is almost least of the Great Lakes, far less
than the sea, which is dandled endlessly by the moon —
this frail, wan moon in the cloud keep.
Here on this December beach, water and the dark
engulf (I am no Hemingway)
and gratefulness goes up like smoke from altars
for this clean, well-lighted place.

Sister M. Davida

BEYOND DESERVING

I do not ask assuagement of my hunger,
(At least not now nor here)
I beg no drink that would allay
My thirst (tomorrow I may fear
Such strict and so appropriate renouncement).

This hour and in this place I pray
Only to thirst and thirst again, only to hunger
Still after a surfeiting that is divine,
Knowing such craving is beyond deserving
And it were graceless certainly for me
To seek fulfillment forwardly.

Sister M. Paulinus

THE QUOTIDIAN IN CUT GLASS

I

In the greyness planes dissolve to droning.
What humming echoes through the lonely valleys.
A lonely crone is crooning as she spins out miles of mist
    for dissolving planes at midnight in the mountains.

II

Puddles mirror brilliant silk umbrellas.
A million mirrors daze the drowning city.
Mermaids, queens, and princesses snarl the evening
        traffic
    as they pose before the glasses
       and swirl heraldic parasols
          above deep golden wells that the headlights
             drill in anger.

III

The lame deer limps for apples in the orchard
    where a pungent fragrance rises.
Behold! A tall, white surgeon wields his scalpel in the
       moonlight
    and binds the wound with aromatic spices.
Over piles and piles of apples, above the aromatic
       orchard bounds the deer.

IV

Upside down bare trees are growing in the swimming
        pool.
The gardener is washing them with silver simonize
  to guard against the rusts of rainy constellations.

V

Hands that cannot span an octave shake bright motes
      from the piano.
Silver dust and dew dance in the parlor.
A maid is chasing them with brush and feathers.

VI

Cut glass covers crown the jars of candy —
  peppermint and lemon, caramel and mint —
    striped so gorgeously a tiger or a zebra might be
      jealous.
Guard your candy from the zebra and the tiger.
Cover it with cut glass. Guard your cavities.

VII

Now the children's songs arise like azure ribbons.
How they harmonize in turquoise, indigo, cerulean, and
      aqua!
See the carols float and flow in iridescent ribbons —
  in iridescent ribbons and chromatic streams.
How the ribbons float above the flowing streams!

84

VIII

A resplendent purple steward powders now the
      Poconos.
Oh light and sweet as madrigals
  the powder swirls upon the sugared loaves
    and frozen music clings to twig and tree.
The steward puffs his cheeks and bends above a new
      chef-d'œuvre.

IX

The brook beside the cottage in the mountains
  gurgles like a lonely child at play.
A forgotten child is playing with bright pebbles in the
    moonlight
  beside a cottage locked until next June.
Dust and dusters cover chairs and tables; the grown-ups
    are away;
  and only deer come near to hear this lovely tune.

X

Welcome home the wartime prisoner.
Hurl spring at him. Cover him with kisses.
Parade lilac and forsythia; kildeer, finch and robin.
Oh, welcome him to life, proud parents, brothers,
    sisters,
  wistful bairns and wife;
    and let his hound drool doubtful recognition.

XI

There's a deer, and there is one, and there, and there.
　　But where?
One looks, but each time fails
　　except for shaking twigs, a shade, or flashing tails.
Well, there's a deer, right there beside the road.
His blood is bright and spattered on the car ahead.
A deer is seen so easily when he is dead.

XII

Willow and water and wysteria
　　with highlights of sun on froth and forsythia —
These glimmered by on our way to the city.
Torrents of taxicabs, roaring foul ditties,
　　washed away willow and sunlit forsythia.
Weep for wysteria, wrecked by hysteria!
　　Lord, what a pity!

XIII

Lamplights on the campus preen their halos.
Golden waves, centrifugal, are pressing back the
　　　　darkness.
On the campus crowds of saints are congregating.
Glory, Glory Hallelujah! Holiday tomorrow!

XIV

Soft spring air comes on like Christ the Healer.
Unseen comes Christ and gently stirs our hearts
 and whispers, "Rise! Arise!"
We breathe the pristine dawn of resurrection.
Hosannah to the Christ, Eternal Springtime!

Sister M. Davida